THE AMERICAN GIRLS

COOKBOOK

A Peek at Dining in the Past with Meals You Can Cook Today

PLEASANT COMPANY

PICTURE CREDITS

Pages 3, 4, 9, 21—Taken from *Food on the Frontier: Minnesota Cooking from 1850 to 1900, With Selected Recipes*, by Marjorie Kreidberg, © 1975, Minnesota Historical Society; 8, 37—Clarence P. Hornung, *Handbook of Early Advertising Art*, (Dover Publications, Inc., New York, 1947); 11, 15—Early Settler Life Series, Crabtree Publishing Company, New York; 12—North Wind Picture Archives, Alfred, Maine; 48, 51 (bottom), 53, 58, 61—Reproduced with the permission of General Mills, Inc.; 49, 57—Westinghouse Electric Corporation; 50 (top), 51 (top), 55—Courtesy *Coupon Cookery*, Prudence Penny, © 1943 by Hearst Publications; 50 (bottom)—State Historical Society of Wisconsin; 52—*Your Victory Lunch Box*, © 1943 by Dell Publishing Co., Inc.

Written and Edited by Jeanne Thieme
Recipes developed by F. Lynn Nelson and Jeanne Thieme
Designed and Art Directed by Kathleen Brown
Illustration by Luann Roberts
Photography by Scott Lanza
Picture Research by Robyn Hansen

Library of Congress Cataloging-in-Publication Data

The American girls cookbook: a peek at dining in the past with meals you can cook today.

p. cm.—(Portfolio of pastimes)
Summary: Describes the preparation and serving of foods during three time periods in
American history: 1854, 1904, and 1944. Includes recipes for breakfast, lunch, and dinner meals.
ISBN 0-937295-59-0
1. Cookery—Juvenile literature. [1. Cookery, American. 2. United States—Social life and customs—19th century.
3. United States—Social life and customs—20th century. 4. Literary cookbooks.]
I. Series.
TX652.5.A45 1989 641.5'123—dc20 89-34582
CIP   AC

WHAT'S COOKING?

Cooking, dining, and kitchen cleanup were more than pastimes for American girls in times past. On the frontier in 1854, making all the family's meals was the biggest job girls and women had. Every day, Kirsten worked with her mother in their tiny log-cabin kitchen. She fed wood to the fire in the cookstove and hauled water from the creek when it was time to wash dishes.

By the turn of the century, when Samantha was growing up, new kitchen equipment made cooking faster and easier. Samantha's house had a kitchen sink with running water, a new gas stove, and an early kind of refrigerator called an *icebox*. But Samantha didn't use them often. In 1904, servants cooked for wealthy American families. A proper young lady's place was in the dining room, where she learned to be the perfect hostess at elegant formal meals.

Molly's kitchen was much like a kitchen today—except the only dishwasher in it was Molly! During World War Two, most children on the home front helped with *KP* or Kitchen Patrol, the army word for cleanup. Many American women had jobs outside their homes, so they recruited their children to help out in the kitchen.

Some things have changed since The American Girls were growing up. Today's kitchens are equipped with electric dishwashers, microwave ovens, and garbage disposals. Supermarkets sell ready-to-serve frozen foods. And women and girls aren't the only

KIRSTEN ❤ 1854

Kirsten Larson was a pioneer. She lived in a one-room log cabin on the Minnesota frontier. Each morning she helped cook a hearty farm breakfast on the wood-burning stove.

SAMANTHA 🫖 1904

Samantha Parkington was raised by her wealthy grandmother at the turn of the century. She enjoyed a six-course meal in an elegant dining room when the butler announced "dinner is served."

MOLLY ★ 1944

Molly McIntire grew up on America's home front during World War Two. She packed her schoolday lunch with patriotic purpose.

THE AMERICAN GIRLS

CONTENTS

ones who work in the kitchen. Men and boys cook, too. However, other things have stayed exactly the same for American families. We still enjoy hearty breakfasts, elegant dinners, and lunches packed with pep—the same kind of meals Kirsten, Samantha, and Molly ate with their families in times past.

Pioneer families like Kirsten's ate what they could grow on their frontier farms or gather in the woods nearby. There were no supermarkets in 1854. Instead, pioneers planted and harvested their own grain for bread and cereal. They got milk, butter, and cheese from cows or goats they raised themselves. Eggs came from their own chickens. Each fall when they butchered, there was fresh meat. But in the winter, when their hens stopped laying eggs and the cows didn't give milk, pioneer families didn't have those foods to eat. Kirsten and Mama cooked foods like bread and porridge again and again because the ingredients were common on the frontier. They didn't read cookbooks to learn new recipes, and they rarely planned special meals because time for that was scarce. But sometimes there were treats—especially on holidays.

Samantha's everyday meals would have seemed like holiday feasts to Kirsten. When Samantha was a girl, lots of food was served at every proper meal. But the most lavish meals were planned when company came to dinner. When a wealthy lady like Grandmary invited guests, she and her cook worked out the menu days before the dinner party. That gave the cook time to order special foods from the grocer. Canned food was popular at the turn of the century, and fresh vegetables and meat could be shipped across America in trains. In 1904, the country's growing factories were making lots of kitchen gadgets, too. Cookbooks had a place in the kitchen *and* the parlor, because elegant hostesses and their cooks were interested in all the latest recipes. Some cookbooks also gave advice about proper behavior, or **etiquette**, in the dining room.

In 1944, Americans on the home front were more concerned with winning World War Two than with dining on elegant meals. They were proud to be practical in the kitchen. When Mom and Molly cooked, they knew that food was a valuable resource, and they didn't waste it. They found ways to use less meat, sugar, butter, and eggs, which were scarce during the war. They cooked lots of fresh vegetables from their Victory garden. And they read cookbooks for advice about planning healthy meals that were full of important vitamins—including the imaginary vitamin Z for Zest.

Learning about kitchens and cooking in the past will help you understand what it was like to grow up the way American girls like Kirsten, Samantha, and Molly did. Cooking the meals they ate in your own kitchen will bring history alive for you and your family.

The next two pages explain a few things that every good cook should know. In times past, mothers taught them to their daughters. Today, you can read them by yourself. But don't work alone in the kitchen. Cooking together is a tradition American girls and their mothers have always shared. Keep it alive today!

CONTENTS

MEASURING

A good cook measures exactly. Here is a hint for measuring flour.

Spoon the flour into a measuring cup, heaping it up over the top. Then use the spoon handle to level the flour off. Don't shake or tap the cup.

*Sifting makes flour lighter by mixing it with air, so be sure to measure flour **after** you sift it when a recipe calls for sifted flour. Measure first, **then** sift, if the recipe says "1 cup flour, sifted."*

SIXTEEN TIPS FOR SERIOUS COOKS

 *1.* Choose a time that suits your mother, so that you will both enjoy working together in the kitchen.

2. Wash your hands with soap before you handle food. Wear an apron, tie back your hair, and roll up your sleeves.

3. Read a recipe carefully, all the way through, before you start it. Look at the pictures. They will help you understand the tricky steps.

4. Gather all the ingredients and equipment you will need *before* you start to cook. Put everything where you can reach it easily.

5. Clean up spills right away.

6. It pays to be careful. Ask an adult to show you how to chop, slice, and peel with sharp kitchen tools. Don't use the stove or the oven without permission or supervision.

7. Pay attention while using knives so that you don't cut your fingers! Always use a chopping board to save kitchen counters. Remember, a good sharp knife is safer than a dull one.

8. When you stir or mix, hold the bowl or pan steady on a flat surface, not in your arms.

9. Make sure your mixing bowls, pots, and pans are the right size. If they are too small, you'll probably spill. If they are too large, foods will burn more easily.

10. Pans will be less likely to spill on the stove if you turn the handles toward the back.

11. Turn off the stove or the oven as soon as a dish is cooked.

12. Pot holders and oven mitts will protect you from burns. Use them when you touch anything hot. Protect kitchen counters by putting trivets, hotpads, or cooling racks under hot pots and pans.

13. Keep hot foods hot and cold foods cold. If you plan to make things early and serve them later, store them properly. Food that could spoil belongs in a refrigerator. Wrap everything well.

14. Arrange food nicely. Pretty plates make things taste better.

15. Cleanup is part of cooking, too. Leave the kitchen at least as clean as you found it. Wash all the dishes, pots, and pans. Put them back in their proper places when they're dry. Sweep the floor. Throw away the garbage.

16. If you and your mother decide to make a whole meal, be sure to plan so that all the food will be ready when you are ready to serve it. But you don't have to make everything on the menu all at once to get a taste of the way Kirsten, Samantha, and Molly ate!

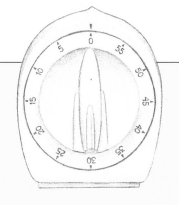

TIMING

When a recipe gives two cooking times—for example, when it says "bake 25 to 30 minutes"—first set the timer for the earliest time. If the food is not done when the timer rings, give it more time.

Not all stoves and ovens are the same. Your mother or another adult can help you learn if yours is hotter or cooler than average. If it's hotter, watch carefully so things don't burn. Use a lower temperature or check foods a few minutes before they are supposed to be done. If it's cooler, raise the temperature or allow things to cook a little longer.

TABLE OF MEASUREMENTS

3 teaspoons = 1 tablespoon

2 cups = 1 pint

2 pints = 1 quart

4 cups = 1 quart

Chapter One
KIRSTEN'S BREAKFAST

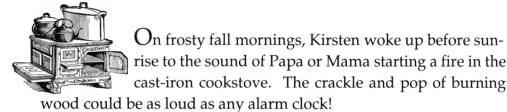

On frosty fall mornings, Kirsten woke up before sunrise to the sound of Papa or Mama starting a fire in the cast-iron cookstove. The crackle and pop of burning wood could be as loud as any alarm clock!

Kirsten didn't wait in bed until she heard the sizzle of frying sausage or sniffed coffee boiling on the stove. She got up right away because she had a job to do. It was time to help Mama cook breakfast—the hearty meal that started a hungry pioneer family's day.

Breakfast had to be served quickly in the dark fall and winter months, when precious hours of daylight slipped away fast. So Kirsten hurried to put on flannel petticoats, her warmest dress, and a work apron. Then she went straight to the stove. If it was so cold that she could see her breath inside the house, she stopped for a moment to wrap a shawl around her shoulders. She wore it until the tiny cookstove had made the whole cabin toasty warm.

As Papa fed the animals, Kirsten and Mama fed wood to the stove so that they could fry fresh pork sausage and boil eggs and coffee. Creamy rice porridge was a special breakfast treat that was waiting in the oven. It had stayed warm all night beside a low-burning fire. Even in 1854, Americans had some convenience foods!

One thing Kirsten ate isn't common on breakfast tables today. She topped off her meal with a cookie, then slipped another into her pocket for a mid-morning snack. Dinner at noon was a long way off!

MENU

Pioneer Breakfast
Autumn 1854

Hard-Boiled Eggs
with Pork Sausage
•
Swedish Rice Porridge
•
Round Rye Bread
•
Homemade Butter
•
Jam, Honey, and Preserves
•
Cheese
•
Ginger Cookies
•
Hot Coffee and Hot Milk

A Swedish-American Meal

PIONEER PANTRIES

*Pioneers didn't have modern re-frigerators or the electricity to run them, but they did have other ways to keep their food from spoiling. Milk and butter for the day and bread for the week were all kept in the **pantry**. Sometimes pantries were small rooms or closets where food, cooking pots, and baking pans were stored. In one-room log cabins like Kirsten's, a few shelves made a pantry. They were covered by a curtain that protected food from cookstove ashes and kept flies off of it in warm weather.*

Kirsten was an immigrant from Sweden, so her breakfast had a Swedish flavor. When immigrants made new homes for themselves in America, they didn't forget their old recipes and customs.

A common Swedish breakfast food was a hot cereal called **gröt** *(grurt)*. Gröt was a porridge like oatmeal, except it was usually made from other grains. Mama often made it with rye or barley the Larsons grew themselves. But sometimes for a special treat, she made **Skånsk gröt** (<u>skone-sk grurt</u>) using store-bought rice and sugar. It tasted like rice pudding! There were apples and raisins in Skånsk gröt. Kirsten had picked the apples from wild apple trees in the woods. She had helped Mama dry wild Minnesota grapes to make raisins. But the smell of them cooking together with the creamy rice made Kirsten remember happy times in Sweden. The recipe for Skånsk gröt came from **Skåne** (<u>skone-ah</u>), the part of Sweden that Kirsten had once called home.

Fried pork was breakfast food for almost every frontier family, no matter where they were from. Most pioneers raised pigs that they butchered in the fall. The Larsons made pork sausage from some of their meat. Most of the sausage was stuffed into casings and dried or smoked so that it wouldn't spoil. But for a few days after butchering, the Larsons had fresh sausage patties to eat.

Butchering was work for both men and women on the frontier. Children often had the job of gathering eggs, a good breakfast food when the hens were laying. In 1854, boiled eggs were served in Swedish-American homes. The table was set with one egg at each place. Kirsten's egg was hard-boiled. She peeled it at the table and cut it into slices before she ate it. Soft-boiled eggs were eaten with bread for dipping up the runny yellow yolk.

In America, the Larson family ate the same kinds of bread they had eaten in Sweden—hard, crisp flatbreads and dark, sturdy loaves of rye. Kirsten and Mama baked bread together at least once a week. They made as many as a dozen loaves at a time. On their bread, American farm families ate butter and cheese that they made from cow's or goat's milk. Sometimes a lucky pioneer girl like Kirsten found wild honey in the woods. That was good on bread, too. And Kirsten ate lots of jam and preserves made from fruit that grew wild on the frontier. By late autumn, most of the berries in the woods were frozen. Jam and berries preserved in sugar were the only fruits pioneers had all winter long.

Papa and Mama couldn't imagine breakfast without a pot of coffee. Children drank coffee with lots of hot milk. But some parents said hot milk sprinkled with cinnamon was better for children. Either beverage was good with a spicy ginger cookie. That's what Kirsten ate at the end of her meal, when her workday had just begun.

1. Leg.
2. Hind Loin.
3. Fore Loin.
4. Spare Rib.
5. Hand.
6. Spring.

BUTCHERING

*Pioneers butchered pigs and cows to get meat, but they found ways to use every bit of an animal. The fat was **rendered** to make lard for cooking and soap. Brains were fried in lard and eaten as an autumn breakfast treat. Pigskin was tanned to make leather. Bristles made brushes. Intestines were cleaned and used for sausage casings.*

Swedish cooks used cow's blood to make a favorite bread. Blood bread was cut into cubes and cooked in hot milk, then served for breakfast.

FRONTIER RECIPES

Most recipes from the 1850s are hard for today's cooks to follow because of the way they measure ingredients—"a pinch" of salt, "a thimble full" of cinnamon, a "dust" of flour, a "squeeze" of lemon, a "handful" of rice, or a lump of butter "the size of an egg." There are instructions to "bake all day" that do not say how hot the oven should be. With directions like that, it's no wonder that cookbooks weren't very common in frontier kitchens! It was much easier for girls to learn to cook as they worked beside their mothers, who could show them exactly what to do.

COOKING AND KITCHENS

In the morning, everyone in Kirsten's family was in a hurry to start the day's work. Kirsten and Mama cooked pioneer "fast food" so that they could serve breakfast quickly. It wasn't like our fast food today!

Much of the Larson family's breakfast was cooked long before the morning it was served. Bread and cookies were baked days earlier and stored on pantry shelves. (Some pioneers didn't think it was healthy to eat bread fresh from the oven.) Kirsten and Mama even made porridge the day before they served it. They cooked it in the afternoon, while the stove was hot and the kitchen was light. At night, they put it in the oven beside a low-burning, or **banked**, fire. By morning it was still warm, and extra thick.

When Kirsten went to bed, breakfast eggs were already in a pan of water on top of the stove, waiting for a hot fire to start them boiling in the morning. Freshly-ground coffee was in the pot. Even sausage patties were shaped and ready to fry. They wouldn't spoil overnight in the cold cabin. But they were covered to keep mice away!

Kirsten and Mama didn't serve "fast food" for breakfast only because everyone was in a hurry. They made breakfast as simple as they could because they had to cook it in the dark. At daybreak, it wasn't bright and sunny in the Larsons' kitchen. Their two small windows were covered with cloth to keep out the cold, and tallow lamps gave off a low, smoky light. So the more things Kirsten and

Mama had ready, the easier breakfast was to make.

The Larsons ate breakfast in the kitchen—which was also the dining room, the living room, and the only bedroom in their one-room log cabin. In winter months, it was nice to have the table near the hot cookstove. But when the weather got warmer, the little cabin was very hot and stuffy whenever Kirsten and Mama cooked because the cookstove also heated the Larsons' house. By summertime, they had to move the stove to an outdoor summer kitchen.

Wood was the only thing Mama could use to control the cookstove's temperature. There were no On/Off switches or knobs marked "low," "medium," and "high." If Mama needed lots of heat on top of the stove, she burned dry oak or another hardwood. If she wanted to bake something slowly, she used less wood, or green wood, or a softer wood like birch to keep the oven temperature lower. Of course, a cooler oven—one that baked bread without burning—meant that Mama had to wait a long time for water to boil on top of the stove.

One of the first things Kirsten learned about cooking was how to feed the fire in the stove. Mama taught her rules about wood and passed along hints for judging oven temperatures without a thermometer. For example, the oven was just right for baking bread when Kirsten could hold her bare hand inside and count to twenty, but no higher. Since there were no kitchen timers to show when things were done, a good cook learned when to check and always kept her mind on the stove.

KITCHEN CLEANUP

*One of the hardest things about frontier cooking was cleanup. There was no running water in log cabins like Kirsten's. Instead, children had the job of hauling water from the well or a nearby stream. In winter, water sometimes froze and ice had to be melted in a basin on the stove. Dishwater had to be heated on the stove, too. There were no detergents. Pioneers used soap made from lard and **lye**, which came from stove ashes. Sometimes they scoured pans with sand or with brushes they made from birch twigs.*

SWEDISH TABLE GRACE

For Kirsten's family, a meal was not a social event. Kirsten might not speak at all, except to say grace along with Papa. Of course, she would answer if Papa or Mama asked her a question.

The Larsons might have used this Swedish table prayer before each meal. It means "May God bless the food we eat."

Välsigna Gud den mat vi få.

(Vel-sing-nuh Goodt den maht vee foh.)

SETTING KIRSTEN'S TABLE

There was no fancy centerpiece on Kirsten's breakfast table. In fact, there were not even matching dishes. The Larsons thought they were lucky to have enough cups and knives so that no one had to share!

Some of the plates and bowls they used came all the way from Sweden. They borrowed a few from Aunt Inger, who lived next door. Papa bought one metal plate at the general store in town. He and Lars, Kirsten's older brother, carved the rest from wood. They carved wooden spoons for cooking and eating, too.

Mama could weave beautiful linen cloth on her loom, but often there wasn't a tablecloth on the smooth wooden table. Pioneers like Kirsten and her family rarely used napkins, either. Laundry was a difficult chore, so cloth napkins were impractical. Paper ones hadn't been invented in 1854.

A few minutes before breakfast was ready, Kirsten called her brothers and Papa, who had already started their work outside. As the menfolk came in to wash up, Kirsten and Mama put the food on the table, poured coffee, and put one egg at each place.

After Papa said grace, the Larsons helped themselves to a hearty meal of porridge, sausage, bread, cheese, butter, honey, and preserves. People ate what they liked, taking whatever looked best to them that morning. But even Kirsten's little brother Peter saved the cookies as a sort of dessert, eating one at the end of the meal and saving another for a snack.

HARD-BOILED EGGS

Ingredients		Equipment
6 large eggs	Salt	1-quart saucepan
Cold water	Pepper	

Directions   **6 servings**

1. Put unshelled <u>eggs</u> in the saucepan and cover them with cold <u>water</u>. *Tip: If the eggs have come right out of the refrigerator, add a teaspoon of salt and a few drops of vinegar to the water. It will keep them from cracking.*

2. Place the pan over medium heat. As soon as the water begins to

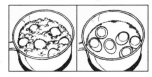

boil, turn the heat down. Simmer the eggs for 15 minutes. *Tip: When water boils, big bubbles rise to the top and burst. When it simmers, you will see only a few tiny bubbles along the sides of the pan.*

3. Take the pan to the sink and place it under cold running water.

When the pan has filled with water that is cool enough to touch, remove the eggs. *Tip: Cold water stops the eggs from cooking and makes them easier to peel.*

4. Dry the shells and place one egg on each plate at the table.

5. Shell your egg at the table, the way Kirsten did. Cut it in slices

and season it with <u>salt</u> and <u>pepper</u>. *Tip: To shell a hard-boiled egg, tap it lightly against a hard surface until it is shattered all around. Then gently peel off the shell. Try using the side of your thumb.*

HARD-BOILED EGGS

Kirsten sliced her egg and ate it with fresh pork sausage.

Today, you can buy frozen sausage patties that taste like the ones Kirsten ate on the frontier. Pioneers didn't have electric freezers, but they sometimes kept meat frozen during the cold winter months. An outdoor shed or a corner of the cabin far from the stove was a frontier freezer.

SWEDISH RICE PORRIDGE

A favorite food, known as Skånsk gröt in Sweden, made Kirsten feel at home in America.

Kirsten and Mama cooked porridge in the afternoon, long before breakfast. A banked fire in the oven kept it warm all night.

SWEDISH RICE PORRIDGE

Ingredients

1 large firm apple
1 teaspoon butter
1 cup rice
1 cup water
3-inch cinnamon
   stick

4 cups milk
3 tablespoons sugar
1/3 cup raisins
1 teaspoon vanilla

Equipment

Vegetable peeler
Apple corer or
   knife
3-quart saucepan
   with cover
Measuring cups
   and spoons
Wooden spoon
   for stirring

Directions

6 servings

1. Peel the <u>apple</u>.
Tip: Use a vegetable peeler. Always peel away from yourself.

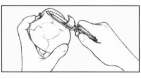

2. Cut out the core and chop the rest of the apple into small pieces. Set it aside.
Tip: You can use a special tool for coring and slicing apples. If you don't have one, use a small knife. Don't forget a cutting board when you chop!

3. Coat the bottom of the saucepan with <u>butter</u>.
Tip: Use your fingers to rub butter over the bottom of the pan. It will keep the rice from sticking as it cooks—and make cleanup easier!

4. Put the <u>rice</u>, <u>water</u>, and <u>cinnamon stick</u> in the saucepan. Place the pan over medium heat. When the water begins to boil, lower the heat and cover the pan. Simmer the rice 10 to 15 minutes, or

until the water has been absorbed.

Tip: Large bubbles will rise to the top and burst when water boils. There will be only a few tiny bubbles when it simmers—but rice will cook better if you don't peek.

5. Pour the <u>milk</u> into the saucepan. Stir. Cook until the milk be-

gins to simmer.

Tip: If you add warm milk, your porridge will cook faster. You will see very tiny bubbles along the edges of the pan when the mixture begins to simmer.

6. When the milk begins to simmer, add the <u>sugar</u>, <u>chopped</u>

<u>apple</u>, and <u>raisins</u>. Stir gently.

Tip: Slip the apple and raisins into the pan so that the porridge doesn't splash.

7. Cover the pan and allow the porridge to simmer for about 45 minutes. As it cooks, it will thicken. *Tip: You may peek at the cooking porridge and give it a stir once or twice.*

8. Turn off the heat and take the pan from the stove. Remove the cinnamon stick. Stir in the <u>vanilla</u>.

9. Pour the porridge into a pretty bowl. Serve it warm with cream or honey.

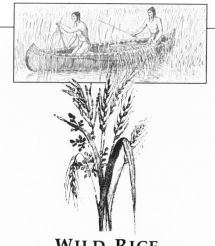

WILD RICE

*In Minnesota wild rice was a **staple**, or one of the basic foods, in Native American diets. Women from the Chippewa and Dakota tribes gave wild rice to families like Kirsten's in exchange for milk and butter. But in 1854, the strong flavor of wild rice wasn't popular with most white settlers. They preferred white rice that was grown on plantations in South Carolina. It was sold in frontier stores.*

ROUND RYE BREAD

Fennel seeds add a hint of licorice flavor to this sweet Swedish brown bread.

---

*Pioneers made bread with home-made yeast. **Spook yeast** was made from mashed potatoes, sugar, salt, and warm water. Other yeasts were made from a plant called hops.*

ROUND RYE BREAD

Ingredients		Equipment
1-1/4 cups milk	3 cups rye flour	Small saucepan
2 packages dry yeast	1 tablespoon	Yeast thermometer
2 tablespoons	salad oil	Measuring cups
soft butter	Extra oil and rye	and spoons
1/2 cup dark	flour for the	Mixing bowl
brown sugar	baking sheet	Wooden spoon
1 tablespoon ground	Butter	Kitchen towel
fennel seed		Baking sheet
1 teaspoon salt		Fork
1 cup white flour		Wire cooling rack

Directions   *1 loaf*

1. Warm the <u>milk</u> over low heat. When the thermometer reading is between 110° and 115°, pour <u>1/2 cup milk</u> into the mixing bowl.
Tip: The correct temperature is very important. Milk that is too hot will destroy the yeast. Milk that is too cold will not "activate" yeast, or make it work.

2. Sprinkle the <u>yeast</u> over the milk in the mixing bowl. Stir well. Set the bowl aside for 3 to 4 minutes, or until the mixture begins to

bubble and swell.
Tip: This is called "proofing" the yeast, or testing it to make sure it is active. Some cooks add a pinch of sugar when they proof yeast.

3. While yeast is proofing, cut the <u>butter</u> into small pieces and add it to the warm <u>milk</u> left in the saucepan. Stir to help the butter melt.
Tip: Small pieces of butter will melt faster than a large chunk.

4. When the yeast has proofed, add the milk and melted butter from the saucepan. Stir in the <u>brown sugar</u>, <u>fennel</u>, and <u>salt</u>. Add the <u>white flour</u> and stir to mix the ingredients.

5. Gradually mix in 2 cups of <u>rye flour</u>. The dough will be very stiff and sticky. Add enough of the <u>remaining rye flour</u> so that you

can shape the dough into a ball.
Tip: Do not add all of the remaining flour. You'll need some for Step 7.

6. Cover the mixing bowl with a towel and let the dough rest in a warm spot for 10 or 15 minutes. *Tip: Yeast must stay warm to keep active. Keep the bowl away from drafts. Put it in a warm, sunny corner or a cool oven. (Don't turn the oven on though, or it will be too hot.)*

7. Take the dough out of the bowl and place it on a table or counter that has been sprinkled with more of the <u>remaining flour</u>. Dust your hands with flour and knead the dough. Whenever the dough begins to stick to your hands, dust them with more flour and sprinkle a little more flour on the dough. By the time you have used the last of the remaining flour, the dough should not be sticky.

8. After 5 to 10 minutes of kneading, you will have a smooth and elastic ball of dough. Cover it with the towel and let it rest while you wash and dry the mixing bowl. *Tip: If you have kneaded the dough enough, it will spring back when you poke it with your finger.*

Recipe continues on page 18.

HOW TO KNEAD BREAD

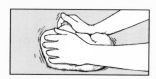

1. Push the heels of your hands down into the dough and away from you.

2. Fold the dough in half.

3. Turn the dough.

4. Push the dough again. Repeat these steps. They will soon become simple, and your kneading will have a rhythm.

BAKING TOOLS

Pioneer cooks didn't have time to bake bread one loaf at a time. Kirsten and Mama made enough to feed a family of five for at least a week—and they served bread at every meal and for snacks, too. Many pioneer women mixed their bread in huge flat bowls carved from logs. They shaped the loaves in straw baskets woven from grass. They made round loaves so that they didn't need bread pans for baking. A family like Kirsten's would have used a dozen pans!

9. Coat the inside of the bowl with the <u>oil</u>. Put the dough in the bowl. Roll it around until it is completely coated with oil. Cover

the bowl with the towel and set it in a warm, draft-free place to rise.

Tip: Coating the dough with oil keeps it from drying out and cracking as it rises.

10. After about 45 minutes, check the dough. It should be double in bulk—twice as big as it was before rising. Test by poking it with your finger. If the dough does *not* spring back, it is ready to be shaped. *Tip: Rising times can change with the weather and the kind of flour you use. If your dough hasn't doubled in bulk after 45 minutes, give it more time. Check it again every 15 minutes.*

11. Oil the baking sheet. Sprinkle it with a little rye flour.

12. Punch the dough in the bowl once or twice, then shape it into a round loaf about 7 inches across. Place it on the baking sheet, cover it with the towel, and let it rise again for 45 minutes.

13. Preheat the oven to 375°. Pierce the loaf all over with a fork.

Make a deeper hole in the center by rotating the fork.

Tip: This is a traditional Swedish shape for bread.

14. Place the baking sheet on the middle rack of the oven. Bake the bread for 50 to 60 minutes. When the top is brown and the loaf sounds hollow when you tap it with your knuckles, remove the bread from the oven and place it on a rack to cool.

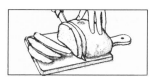

15. While the loaf is still warm—but not hot enough to burn you—rub the top with <u>butter</u>.
Tip: After 2 or 3 hours, the bread is good for slicing.

Lard Rendering Kettle

SHORTENING

*Pioneer cooks didn't bake bread or cookies with their best butter. Fresh butter took too long to make. Old butter that wouldn't keep much longer was sometimes used for baking. But it was much more common to use **lard**, a shortening made from melted-down animal fat. There was no margarine or vegetable shortening in 1854.*

Pioneers made lard when they butchered. They also saved the fat from frying bacon and sausage. They used fat for baking and some-times ate it, or lard, on bread. Of course, they ate butter on bread, too.

JAMS AND PRESERVES

Kirsten and Mama made all of the jams and preserves the Larson family ate. They used wild fruit from the woods and sugar from the store. Strawberry, raspberry, blackberry, grape, and plum preserves were all favorites on the Minnesota frontier.

CHEESE

Pioneer girls and women made cheese from the milk their cows gave. Hard cheese like Cheddar took several days to make. It could be stored for a long time. Cottage cheese was quicker to make, but it spoiled more easily.

You can get Cheddar and cottage cheese for your pioneer breakfast at the store. Slice the Cheddar and put the cottage cheese in a bowl. Eat either cheese on sliced bread.

HOMEMADE BUTTER

You don't need a churn to make enough rich, creamy butter for breakfast.

———— ❦ ————

Kirsten and Mama made butter once a week. Their cream came from the Larson family's cows. Pioneer women sometimes sold or traded butter at the general store in town.

HOMEMADE BUTTER

Ingredients	Equipment	
2 cups heavy whipping cream, chilled	2-quart jar with tight lid	2-quart bowl
Cold water	1 marble	Wooden spoon
Pinch of salt	Fine sieve	Butter mold

Directions   *6 ounces*

1. Chill the jar and the marble in the refrigerator for at least 1 hour.
Tip: Chilled cream and cold equipment help butter form more quickly.

2. Place the sieve over the bowl. Set them aside.

3. Pour the <u>cream</u> into the jar, drop in the marble, and fasten the lid tight.

4. Shake the jar. At first you will hear the marble moving. After about 15 minutes, the cream will get so thick that you won't hear or feel the marble. The sides of the jar will be coated with thick cream.

Tip: If your arm gets tired, have a partner shake the jar for a while. How long you will have to shake depends upon the temperature, how old the cream is, and how fast or slowly you shake.

5. Continue shaking the jar. After another 15 to 30 minutes, butter will begin to form. First you will hear the marble moving again. Then the coating of cream will disappear from the sides of the jar and you will see lumps of butter in a milky liquid. The liquid is buttermilk. *Tip: The lumps of butter will be at least as thick as your finger.*

6. Open the jar and pour the butter and the buttermilk through the sieve. Then empty the buttermilk from the bowl. Rinse the bowl with cold <u>water</u>.

Tip: If you don't want to drink your buttermilk, be like a thrifty pioneer and save it for making pancakes for another breakfast.

7. Turn the butter out of the sieve and into the bowl. Cover it with cold water, then pour the water off through the sieve. Do not save the milky water. Keep washing the butter this way until the water you pour off is clear. *Tip: You are washing out the buttermilk. Buttermilk that is not washed out will turn the butter sour.*

8. Use a clean wooden spoon to stir and press the butter against the side of the bowl. Work out any liquid that is left in the butter. Pour it off.

Tip: It may be easier to work half of the butter at a time.

9. If you like your butter lightly salted, add a pinch of <u>salt</u> and work it in.

10. Press the butter into a butter mold or a dish. Chill it in the refrigerator for an hour or two. Then unmold and serve with homemade bread.

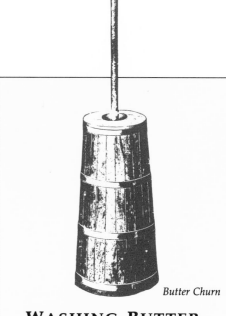

Butter Churn

WASHING BUTTER

The best butter was made with the cleanest tools. Careful pioneers washed their churns carefully and rinsed all of their equipment with boiling water before they made butter. Later, they washed the butter, too. By squeezing out every bit of leftover buttermilk and rinsing the butter again and again, they kept it from turning sour. Finished butter was salted and pressed into plain dishes or carved molds that gave it pretty shapes.

GINGER COOKIES

These thick spicy cookies won't crush in a pocket.

You can use butter, margarine, or vegetable shortening when you bake these cookies. Pioneers like Kirsten often used lard. They stored cookies in the pantry in stoneware jars.

GINGER COOKIES

Ingredients		Equipment
6 cups sifted flour	1/3 cup soft	Measuring cups
2 teaspoons	shortening	and spoon
baking soda	1-1/2 cups dark	Flour sifter
1 teaspoon salt	molasses	2 mixing bowls
1 teaspoon allspice	2/3 cup cold water	Wooden spoon
1 teaspoon ginger	Shortening to grease	Rolling pin
1 teaspoon cloves	baking sheets	Cookie cutters
1 teaspoon cinnamon	Extra flour for	Pancake turner
1 cup brown sugar	rolling out dough	Baking sheets

Directions   *2-1/2 dozen*

1. Sift together the <u>flour</u>, <u>baking soda</u>, <u>salt</u>, <u>allspice</u>, <u>ginger</u>, <u>cloves</u>, and <u>cinnamon</u>. Set the sifted dry ingredients aside in a small mixing bowl. **Tip:** *Remember to sift the flour twice—first before you measure it, and then with the soda, salt, and spices.*

2. Use a wooden spoon to stir and press the <u>brown sugar</u> and <u>shortening</u> together against the side of a large mixing bowl.

 **Tip:** *When you measure brown sugar, pack it tightly into the cup with your fingers. It should keep its shape when you turn it out of the measuring cup.*

3. Add the <u>molasses</u> and <u>water</u>. Stir to mix well.

4. Add the sifted dry ingredients 1 cup at a time. Mix well after each addition. The dough will get very stiff and hard to stir. Keep mixing until all of the dry ingredients disappear.

5. Cover the bowl and chill the dough for 1 hour. *Tip: Chilling makes the dough less sticky and easier to handle. You can cover the bowl with plastic wrap or the way pioneers did—with a large plate.*

6. Preheat the oven to 350°. Lightly grease the baking sheets.
Tip: Use <u>shortening</u>, not butter, which will burn. Spread the shortening with your fingers or with a paper towel.

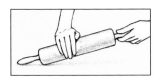

7. Sprinkle some <u>flour</u> onto a table or counter. Cover the rolling pin with flour.
Tip: Flour keeps the dough from sticking. Use more when you need it.

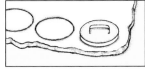

8. Divide the dough into four sections. Roll out the first section 1/2-inch thick. Cut out shapes with cookie cutters.
Tip: Roll from the center of the dough to the edges. Try to keep the whole piece of dough the same thickness.

9. Lift the cookies onto the cookie sheet with the pancake turner. Leave at least 2 inches between cookies, because they get big and puffy as they bake.

10. Make more cookies from the rest of your dough, including the scraps.

11. Bake the cookies 12 to 15 minutes, or until your finger does not leave an imprint when you touch them lightly.

12. Use the pancake turner to remove the cookies from the baking sheets. *Tip: Don't stack the cookies while they are hot, or they will stick together.*

BAKING SODA

*When Kirsten was a girl, baking soda was called **saleratus** (sal-a-<u>rate</u>-us). It sometimes had a harsh chemical flavor. Spices like cinnamon, cloves, and ginger had a stronger flavor than saleratus. That made them popular in baked foods like cookies. Cinnamon, cloves, and ginger also tasted good with molasses—the most common sweetener in pioneer cooking. Sugar was scarce and expensive on the frontier.*

Chapter Two
SAMANTHA'S DINNER

Samantha loved the gleam of silver and the glitter of crystal in Grandmary's candlelit dining room. Dinner was a formal occasion in wealthy homes at the turn of the century, so Samantha practiced her very best manners. She felt quite grown up each time she and her grandmother dined together.

In 1904, American girls like Samantha would *dress for dinner* every evening. If Samantha and Grandmary were alone, they put on nicer dresses than the ones they'd worn in the afternoon. When company came to dinner, they dressed in their best clothes. For the fanciest dinners, women had jewels and elaborate gowns. They even wore gloves into the dining room!

Gentlemen escorted ladies to the table when the butler announced, "Dinner is served." Everyone sat at an assigned place, marked with a name card. Often there was a small menu card, too. People didn't choose from the menu, as you might in a restaurant today. Everything the menu listed—and more—was served. In fact, "everything from soup to nuts" is a good way to describe what was on the menu for a proper turn-of-the-century dinner.

Dinner was served in *courses.* Even the simplest family meal had at least three courses—soup, the main course, and dessert. The fanciest dinners might have as many as eighteen courses. Samantha's dinner for company had six. Like all good turn-of-the-century dinners, it started with soup and ended with nuts!

SAMANTHA

MENU

Dinner for Company
November 1904

1st course
Cream of Carrot Soup
Celery, Radishes, Olives
•

2nd course
Salmon with Lemon Butter
Sliced Cucumbers
•

3rd course
Roasted Beef Tenderloin
Mashed Potatoes   Green Beans
Corn Oysters
•

4th course
French Salad
American Standard Cheese
•

5th course
Ice Cream Snowballs
Dainties
•

6th course
Fresh Fruit
•

Demitasse, Nuts, Raisins

Sardine Serving Box

KICKSHAWS

*All of the courses in an elegant dinner had French names. Sometimes menus were written in French, too. At the turn of the century, knowing the meanings of French words and how to pronounce them was an important social skill. "Kickshaws" was an English way of trying to say a French word for "a little something"—**quelque chose** (kel kah shows).*

Sardines were fashionable kickshaws because they were sold in cans. Canned food was a luxury when Samantha was a girl.

SAMANTHA'S DINNER COURSES

Each course in a turn-of-the-century dinner included several dishes. Samantha's soup course was served with appetizers like celery, radishes, and olives. Appetizers were sometimes called *kickshaws.*

Cucumber slices were part of the fish course. In 1904, wealthy families across America could get cucumbers all year long because during the winter, cucumbers and other fashionable foods were grown in heated glass buildings. Potato chips could be part of a fashionable fish course, too! They were called Saratoga Potatoes when Samantha was a girl.

Roast beef was a favorite food at the turn of the century and the main course in Samantha's dinner. It was served with three side dishes—mashed potatoes, green beans, and corn patties shaped like oysters, another popular food in 1904.

After the main course, Samantha had *punch,* a frozen fruit ice or sherbet. Punch wasn't considered a course. Instead, it was a light refreshment between courses. Punch was never listed on the dinner menu, but it was often served.

The fourth course in Samantha's dinner was salad, cheese, and crackers. In 1904, Cheddar cheese was called American Standard. At more elaborate dinners, a game course of duck or pheasant was served with the salad.

Samantha's fifth course was dessert. At the fanciest dinner parties, two desserts were served—first, an elaborate cake or pudding, then a frozen dessert. After dessert, candies called *bonbons* were passed. Simpler meals for company had just one dessert, and ice cream was a popular choice. It could be served with or without *dainties*, another name for small cakes or cookies.

The last course in Samantha's dinner was fruit. But first, each guest was given a finger bowl. Meals ended with coffee served in tiny cups, or *demitasse*. Raisins, warm salted nuts, and mints were served with coffee.

Since children did not drink coffee when Samantha was a girl, she might have enjoyed hot cocoa at the end of her meal. But there was never a special children's menu for her unless she ate by herself in another room. In 1904, some children had to do just that! Most adults believed that a child who couldn't sit properly, eat the food that was served, use the correct knife and fork, and be entertained by adult conversation didn't belong at the dinner table—especially when company came to dinner. Young ladies like Samantha were welcome, of course.

FINGER BOWLS

Servants brought finger bowls to the table after the dessert course had been cleared. Finger bowls were small, crystal bowls half-full of warm water. Often a thin slice of lemon or a fragrant flower floated on the water.

Finger bowls were served on two plates. The bottom plate was for the fruit course. The smaller crystal plate on top of it held the finger bowl and a napkin. Sometimes it held a chocolate peppermint wafer, too.

Each guest lifted the smaller plate (and the finger bowl) off of the fruit plate and placed it on the table. Guests dipped their fingers, one hand at a time, into their finger bowls and dried them daintily on their napkins.

BUTLERS

Hawkins, the butler, was one of the most respected servants in Grand-mary's house. His biggest job was serving all the meals. He also made sure that meals began on time.

Butlers were in charge of all the servants who worked in the dining room. They polished all the silver and made sure the lamps and candles were in perfect condition. And they kept their pantries immaculately clean.

At night, butlers locked the front door after everyone else had gone to bed. When Samantha was a girl, a butler like Hawkins could earn between $35 and $70 a month.

SERVANTS AND SERVING

Grandmary was the hostess when company came to dinner. She planned the menu, invited guests, and even decided where they would sit. But she could not have entertained without servants.

Mrs. Hawkins, the cook, prepared all of the food. She got help from a scullery maid who did the dishes and helped keep the kitchen clean. A butler and a maid served Samantha's six-course dinner. The butler was in charge. The maid helped him at the table. She also worked in the **butler's pantry**, a small room between the kitchen and the dining room.

The most elegant and elaborate turn-of-the-century dinners were served **Russian style**. Many servants worked in the dining room when dinner was served Russian style. They brought plates to the table the way restaurant waiters do today. Samantha's six-course dinner was certainly elegant, but it was considered a simpler meal in 1904. Simpler meals were served in the very proper but more informal **English style**. At an English-style dinner, the hostess "helped" the servants with their work.

Grandmary "served" the soup after a servant brought it to her in a fancy covered dish called a **tureen**. She put soup into each soup plate, and the servants put soup plates in front of the guests. Even the guests "helped" the servants with their work. They passed kickshaws around the table when they wanted them, or when Grandmary suggested they might.

After the soup course was cleared, servants brought in the fish course and warm plates. A gentleman—Uncle Gard or Admiral Beemis—"served" the fish by putting a portion on each plate. A servant offered everyone sliced cucumbers. Guests who wanted vinegar on their cucumbers served themselves from a small crystal pitcher called a *cruet.*

A gentleman also "served" the main course when he carved the roast. Then one servant placed a plate of sliced meat in front of each guest while the other offered everyone vegetables. After they had cleared the dinner plates, the servants served frozen punch in tiny cups that had been filled in the butler's pantry.

As Grandmary "prepared" the salad by tossing it with dressing, the servants passed out cold salad plates and smaller plates and knives for cheese. They offered everyone a helping of salad. The guests helped themselves to cheese and toasted biscuits, and passed them around the table. Grandmary also "served" dessert with the help of her guests, who passed the plates around the table after she filled them. And the hostess always poured coffee at the end of the meal.

Since the hostess had "served" the food at Samantha's dinner, it was polite for guests to have second helpings and to talk about how good everything tasted. At more formal meals, that was very rude!

SILENT SERVANTS

Servants were expected to be quiet. They did not speak to the guests or to one another when they were in the dining room. The hostess did not speak to the servants, either. Well-trained servants were supposed to know exactly what to do and when to do it. So if a servant was needed, it was more proper for the hostess to ring a tiny silver bell than to call the servant's name. Some dining rooms even had secret buzzers under the table. A hostess tapped the buzzer with her foot to call servants into the dining room without speaking to them.

NAME CARDS

Proper seating was important at turn-of-the-century dinner tables. Ladies always sat at the right of gentlemen. The most important female guest was seated to the right of the host. The most important male guest was seated to the left of the hostess.

Small, simple name cards showed guests where to sit. Menu cards let them know what dishes would be served in each course. The date of the dinner was always given at the top of a menu card.

SETTING SAMANTHA'S TABLE

This is the way etiquette books in 1904 said a proper table should be *laid*, or set.

1. First, cover the table with a felt *silence cloth* to soften the rattle of knives, forks, and dishes. Lay a fine white damask tablecloth over the silence cloth. The center crease of the tablecloth should divide the table exactly in half.

2. Place a white lace or embroidered cloth, called a *centerpiece*, in the middle of the table. On it, place a flower arrangement or the fruit bowl. Place a candlestick at each of the four corners of the centerpiece.

3. Place small silver or crystal dishes of kickshaws and salted nuts exactly between the four candlesticks. Place salt and pepper near the ends of the table or at each place. If you are serving bonbons, you may place them near the centerpiece.

4. Now start to lay the *covers*. Each person's plate, glass, and silverware is a cover. For each cover, allow as much space as the table will permit—not less than twenty inches, but more if possible. At the exact center of the cover, place the *service plate*, a large dinner plate.

5. To the left of the service plate, arrange all of the forks to be used before dessert, in the order they will be used.

6. To the right of the service plate, arrange the knives. All knife blades point toward the plate. The longest and largest knife is nearest the plate. To the right of the knives, place the soup spoon.

7. The foot of the water goblet should just touch the tip of the blade of the longest knife.

8. Place a large white dinner napkin to the left of each service plate. Fold a dinner roll in each napkin.

9. Place a name card above each service plate and a menu card between every two guests.

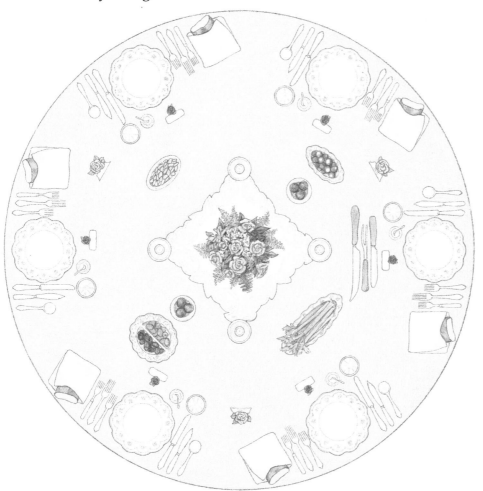

A COVER

The bottom edge of the service plate and all silverware should be one inch from the edge of the table. All other silverware is brought to the table as courses are served.

1. napkin	6. roast knife
2. fish fork	7. fish knife
3. roast fork	8. soup spoon
4. salad fork	9. water goblet
5. service plate	10. salt cellar

CREAM OF CARROT SOUP

*Decorate this creamy orange-colored soup with toast cutouts called **croutons**.*

It's still very proper to serve cream soups in shallow bowls called soup plates.

CREAM OF CARROT SOUP

Ingredients	Equipment	
2 pounds carrots	Vegetable peeler	3-quart saucepan
4 cups chicken broth	Knife and cutting	Measuring cups and
1/4 cup butter	board	spoons
1/4 cup flour	2-quart saucepan	Wooden spoon
1/2 teaspoon salt	Fork	
1/8 teaspoon	Large bowl	
cayenne pepper	Colander	
2 cups half-and-half	Potato masher	

Directions   ***6 servings***

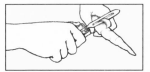

1. Peel the <u>carrots</u> and cut them into 1/2 inch slices.
*Tip: Always move a vegetable peeler **away** from yourself, not toward you. Use a cutting board when you slice.*

2. Put the sliced carrots into the smaller saucepan. Add the <u>chicken broth</u>. Place the pan over medium heat. When the broth begins to boil, turn the heat down to medium-low. *Tip: Bubbles will rise to the top and burst when the broth begins to boil.*

3. Cook the carrots 20 minutes, or until they are very soft. *Tip: The carrots are soft enough if they break apart when you pierce them with a fork.*

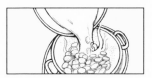

4. Pour the broth from the carrots into the bowl. Set the broth aside.
Tip: Use the colander for this step. Put it over the bowl to catch the carrots.

5. Put the drained carrots back into the saucepan. Mash them with the potato masher until they are soft and smooth.

6. Place the larger saucepan over medium heat. Add the <u>butter</u>. When it melts and sizzles, add the <u>flour</u>. Stir to mix. Then cook

the mixture for 3 to 4 minutes. Stir it often.

Tip: Add the flour all at once. As the mixture cooks, it will turn golden brown. Do not let it burn.

7. Add the <u>mashed carrots</u>, <u>salt</u>, and <u>cayenne pepper</u>. Stir to mix them together.

8. Slowly pour in the <u>broth</u>. Stir until the soup is smooth and bubbly, about 10 minutes.

9. Add the <u>half-and-half</u>. Stir again, and heat the soup slowly. Do not let it boil.

10. Pour hot soup into bowls. Top each serving with croutons. *Tip: If you have a soup tureen, bring the soup to the table and let the hostess fill soup plates there, just as Grandmary would have done.*

BAKED CROUTONS

To make your own croutons, you will need sliced bread, butter, a baking sheet, a butter spreader, and small cookie cutters. Preheat the oven to 400°. Spread butter on both sides of the bread slices, then use cookie cutters to cut each slice into small shapes. Arrange the shapes on the baking sheet. Place it on the center rack of the oven for 5 minutes, or until the shapes are toasty brown on top. Turn them over and bake 5 minutes more.

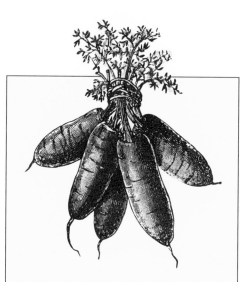

COLORFUL CARROTS

Some rules about what was proper in 1904 seem old-fashioned today. One popular cookbook said plain cooked carrots did not belong on a proper dinner table. Why? Because their orange color was too bright! In 1904, it was more common to use carrots for soups and garnishes.

SALMON WITH LEMON BUTTER

Today, this recipe would be called Poached Salmon. Turn-of-the-century cooks called it Boiled Salmon.

For a fish course like Samantha's, serve half a salmon steak per person. If salmon will be your main course, allow one steak per person.

SALMON WITH LEMON BUTTER

Ingredients	Equipment	
3 salmon steaks, 1-inch thick	10-inch skillet, 2 inches deep, with cover	Warm plate
2 cups water	Measuring cup and spoon	Fork
1 teaspoon salt	Slotted pancake turner	Warm serving platter

Directions   *6 servings*

1. Lay the <u>salmon steaks</u> in the skillet. Add the <u>water</u> and sprinkle with <u>salt</u>.

2. Place the skillet over medium heat. When the water begins to boil, lower the heat and cover the skillet. Cook the fish 7 minutes, or until it flakes with a fork.

Tip: Cook fish over low heat. The water should barely bubble.

3. Lift the cooked salmon from the water. Place it on a warm plate and remove the skin.
Tip: Use a slotted pancake turner to lift the fish.

4. Divide each steak into two pieces and remove the bones.
Tip: Use a fork to loosen the skin and remove the bones. Work quickly, so the salmon doesn't get cold.

5. Place the salmon on a warm serving platter. Serve with lemon-parsley butter. *Tip: It's perfectly proper to serve salmon that has not been skinned and boned. Dinner guests can "help" with this step at the table.*

LEMON-PARSLEY BUTTER		

Ingredients

1 tablespoon
  snipped parsley
1/2 cup butter
1 tablespoon fresh
  lemon juice

Equipment

Kitchen shears   Small saucepan
Sturdy narrow glass Wooden spoon
Measuring cup
  and spoon

Directions

1. To snip <u>parsley</u>, put some fresh parsley leaves into a narrow glass. Cut them in the glass with a kitchen shears.

2. Melt the <u>butter</u> in the saucepan. *Tip: Use low heat. Don't let the butter brown.*

3. Add the <u>lemon juice</u> and snipped parsley. Stir.
Tip: Use a fresh lemon and a juicer for the best lemon juice. Watch out for seeds!

4. Spoon 1 tablespoon of lemon-parsley butter over each piece of salmon.

FISH AND CHIPS

Potato chips could be part of the fish course in a fashionable meal. They were called Saratoga Potatoes in 1904. Saratoga Potatoes were invented at a restaurant in Saratoga Springs, New York, by an American Indian named Pete Francis. When someone complained that the French fries were too thick, Mr. Francis sliced potatoes very thin, fried them in oil, and served them instead.

ROASTED BEEF TENDERLOIN

The center is still pink when this meat is cooked to perfection.

— ❖ —

When turn-of-the-century cooks roasted meat, they baked it in the oven. Pioneer cooks roasted meat over open fires.

ROASTED BEEF TENDERLOIN

Ingredients

2-pound trimmed
  beef tenderloin,
  tied for baking
1 teaspoon salt
1/2 teaspoon pepper

Equipment

Sturdy baking pan
  with 1-inch sides
Aluminum foil
Kitchen shears

Warm serving
  platter
2 forks for lifting
  meat onto platter

Directions   6 servings

1. Preheat the oven to 450°.

2. Sprinkle <u>salt</u> and <u>pepper</u> all over the <u>meat</u>, then put it in the pan.
Tip: Sprinkle the seasoning evenly.

3. Place the pan on the middle rack in the oven. Bake 30 minutes for medium-rare meat, 35 minutes for medium.

4. Remove the pan from the oven and cover the meat with foil. Let it "rest" for 15 minutes.
Tip: The meat keeps on cooking as it rests. Resting makes it easier to cut.

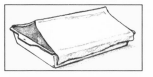
5. Just before serving, uncover the meat. Use kitchen shears to cut the string. Place the meat on a warm serving platter.
Tip: Use 2 forks to lift the meat onto the platter.

6. Carve the meat in the kitchen or at the table.

HOW TO CARVE

At Samantha's very proper dinner, a gentleman "helped" the servants with their work by carving the roast in the dining room. He used a large carving fork and a sharp carving knife. After he had sliced enough meat for everyone, he placed a serving on each dinner plate. Some hostesses in 1904 thought it was old-fashioned to carve at the table. They had their roasts sliced in the kitchen.

Ask the hostess at your dinner where she would like the roast carved. Whether it's in the kitchen or the dining room, make sure an adult uses the sharp carving knife.

There were no electric carving knives in 1904!

1. *Use the fork to hold the roasted meat steady.*

2. *Cut the meat in slices that are 1 inch thick. Use a sawing motion.*

3. *Lift one slice of meat onto each dinner plate.*

SHOPPING FOR FOOD

There were no supermarkets in 1904. Instead, a cook like Mrs. Hawkins bought different kinds of food at different stores. She went to the grocer's for vegetables and to the butcher's shop for meat. A helpful butcher or grocer could be a busy cook's best friend. He would order special foods for her or set aside the best roast when she told him that guests were coming to dinner. He could tie the roast for baking, too.

MASHED POTATOES

*What could be better than pools of
butter melting in mountains of
creamy mashed potatoes?*

— ❧ —

You *can still get potato mashers
like the one Mrs. Hawkins
used in 1904.*

MASHED POTATOES

Ingredients	Equipment	
6 medium potatoes	Vegetable peeler	Measuring cup and
Water	Knife and	spoons
1-1/4 teaspoons salt	cutting board	Fork
1/2 cup milk	2-quart saucepan	Colander
4 tablespoons butter	with cover	Potato masher

Directions   *6 servings*

1. Peel the <u>potatoes</u> and cut them into quarters.
Tip: Move the vegetable peeler away from yourself. Use a cutting board.

2. Put the potatoes in the pan and cover them with <u>water</u>. Add <u>1 teaspoon salt</u>. Cover the pan and place it over medium-high heat. When the water begins to boil, turn the heat down to medium. Let the potatoes boil for 20 minutes, or until they are soft when pricked with a fork. *Tip: Don't boil the potatoes too long, or they will be mushy.*

3. Pour the water from the potatoes. Return the potatoes to the pan.
Tip: Use a colander and work over the sink. Be careful— hot water and steam can burn.

4. Mash the potatoes slightly. Add <u>milk</u>, <u>butter</u>, and <u>1/4 teaspoon salt</u>, then use the potato masher to whip the potatoes until they are light and fluffy.
Tip: You can also use an electric mixer to whip the potatoes.

FRESH GREEN BEANS

Ingredients	Equipment
1-1/2 pounds fresh green beans	1-quart saucepan
1/2 teaspoon salt	Measuring cup and spoon
1 cup water	Colander

Directions

6 servings

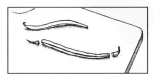

1. Rinse the <u>beans</u> with water, then break off both ends of each bean.
Tip: Breaking off the ends is called "tipping and tailing" the beans. Don't break off too much!

2. Put the beans in the saucepan. Add the <u>salt</u> and just enough <u>water</u> to cover the beans. *Tip: You may not need a whole cup of water.*

3. Place the pan over medium heat. When the water begins to boil, turn the heat down to low. Let the beans simmer for 15 minutes.

Tip: Big bubbles will rise to the top and burst when the water starts to boil. When the beans are simmering, you will see only a few tiny bubbles along the sides of the pan.

4. Pour the water from the beans. Serve them hot, in a pretty bowl.
Tip: When you drain the beans, use a colander and work over the sink. Watch out for falling beans!

FRESH GREEN BEANS

Add color and crunch to the roast course with bright green beans.

In 1904, green beans from California were shipped across America in trains.

CORN OYSTERS

Corn patties in the shape of a fashionable seafood look elegant on the table—and on the menu card.

———— ❦ ————

In 1904, cooks like Mrs. Hawkins didn't have paper towels or aluminum foil in their kitchens.

CORN OYSTERS

Ingredients	*Equipment*	
2 cups frozen corn kernels	Colander	Ovenproof platter
1/4 cup milk	Medium-sized bowl	10-inch skillet
1/3 cup flour	Measuring cups and spoons	Pancake turner
1 egg	Wooden spoon	Aluminum foil
1/2 teaspoon salt	Paper towels	
1/4 teaspoon pepper		
2 tablespoons butter		
2 tablespoons vegetable oil		

Directions   *16 corn oysters*

1. Rinse the frozen <u>corn</u> with water just until the ice crystals disappear.
Tip: Use a colander when you thaw the corn.

2. Place the corn in the bowl. Add the <u>milk</u>, <u>flour</u>, <u>egg</u>, <u>salt</u>, and <u>pepper</u>. Stir to mix.

3. Lay paper towels on top of the platter, then set it aside.

4. Place the skillet over medium heat. Add <u>butter</u> and <u>oil</u>. When the butter melts completely, carefully put 6 rounded spoonfuls of the corn mixture into the skillet.

Tip: Use the stirring spoon to measure out the corn mixture. Avoid dropping the corn oysters into the hot butter and oil. Splatters will burn!

5. Let the corn oysters cook for 2 or 3 minutes, or until the bottoms are golden brown. Then turn them gently. Cook for 2 or 3 minutes

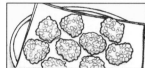 more, or until both sides are golden brown.
Tip: Use the pancake turner to turn the corn oysters.

6. Remove the corn oysters from the skillet. Put them on the paper towel-covered platter to drain. Cover the platter with foil and keep it warm in a 200° oven.

7. Make more corn oysters, repeating Steps 4, 5, and 6 until all of the corn mixture is gone. You should have about 16 corn oysters.

8. Remove the foil and paper towels from the platter and serve corn oysters hot.

FOOD FASHIONS

There are fashions in food just as there are fashions in clothing. When Samantha was growing up, oysters were very fashionable. Raw oysters—six per person—were the first course in many elaborate dinners.

Broccoli had been a fashionable food in some American cities when Kirsten was a girl. But it was unfashionable at the turn of the century. Most cookbooks from Samantha's day did not even mention broccoli. It became fashionable again just before Molly was born.

FRENCH SALAD

Salads were a popular food in 1904. When a menu listed "French Salad," everyone expected lettuce.

---

*If your salad will be tossed at the table, bring out the dressing in a fancy little pitcher, or **cruet**.*

FRENCH SALAD

Ingredients

1 large head
   romaine lettuce
1/4 cup snipped
   chives
1 tablespoon fresh
   tarragon leaves

Equipment

Colander
Paper towels and a
   clean kitchen towel
Kitchen shears
Serving bowl

Measuring cup
   and spoon
Salad tongs or two
   large spoons

Directions

6 servings

1. Break off the <u>lettuce</u> leaves and put them in a colander. Rinse the lettuce with cold, cold water.

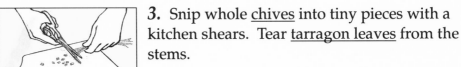

Tip: Check the outer leaves for brown or wilted spots. Don't use the damaged lettuce.

2. Pat the lettuce leaves dry. Tear them into bite-size pieces. Roll the pieces up in a dry kitchen towel. Put the towel in the refrigerator.

Tip: Use paper towels to gently dry the lettuce.

3. Snip whole <u>chives</u> into tiny pieces with a kitchen shears. Tear <u>tarragon leaves</u> from the stems.

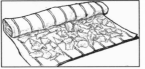

4. Just before you are ready to serve the salad, put the lettuce into the serving bowl. Add the chives and tarragon. Toss the salad

with dressing, using salad tongs or two large spoons.

Tip: Toss the salad gently by lifting it up from the bottom of the bowl until all the pieces are covered with dressing.

DRESSING

Ingredients

3 tablespoons
    tarragon vinegar
1 tablespoon water
1 teaspoon Dijon-
    style mustard
1/2 teaspoon salt

1/2 teaspoon sugar
1/4 teaspoon pepper
1/2 cup vegetable
    or olive oil

Equipment

1-pint jar with cover
Measuring cup
    and spoons

Directions

1. Put the <u>vinegar</u>, <u>water</u>, <u>mustard</u>, <u>salt</u>, <u>sugar</u>, and <u>pepper</u> into the jar. Cover the jar and shake it to blend the ingredients. *Tip: Be sure the jar is covered tightly before you start to shake it.*

2. Add the <u>oil</u>. Put the lid back on the jar and shake it again, hard

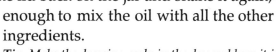

enough to mix the oil with all the other ingredients.

Tip: Make the dressing early in the day and keep it in the jar. Shake it once more before tossing with the salad.

TRAVELING LETTUCE

*Just a few years before Samantha was born, only wealthy Americans ate green salads in the winter months. Fresh lettuce was grown near the city of Boston in heated glass buildings called **hothouses**. It was very expensive.*

*By 1900, many fresh fruits and vegetables came to American cities from California. They traveled on refrigerated railroad cars. But most lettuce was too fragile to travel successfully. Then in 1903, sturdy **iceberg lettuce** was developed. It changed American salad bowls forever.*

ICE CREAM SNOWBALLS

Vanilla ice cream in a coat of shredded coconut.

A cook like Mrs. Hawkins made ice cream by cranking the handle of her ice cream freezer.

ICE CREAM SNOWBALLS

Ingredients	Equipment
1 quart vanilla ice cream	Measuring cup
2 cups shredded coconut	Shallow bowl
12 fancy cookies	Ice cream scoop
	Baking sheet
	2 large spoons
	Plastic wrap

Directions   *6 snowballs*

1. Put the <u>ice cream</u> in the refrigerator for 30 minutes or until it is soft enough to scoop.

2. Put the <u>shredded coconut</u> in the bowl.

3. Scoop out a large ball of ice cream and drop it into the coconut.

4. Roll the ice cream around until it is covered with coconut. Then lift it onto the baking sheet.

Tip: Use two spoons to roll the ice cream and to lift it out of the bowl.

5. Repeat Steps 3 and 4 until you have 6 snowballs.

Tip: Don't let the snowballs touch one another on the baking sheet.

6. Cover the baking sheet with plastic wrap. Freeze the snowballs several hours or overnight. *Tip: Seal plastic wrap tightly so the coconut doesn't dry out.*

7. Take the baking sheet out of the freezer 15 minutes before you are ready to serve dessert. *Tip: Serve snowballs with 1 or 2 fancy <u>cookies</u>.*

THE FRUIT COURSE

Sometimes fresh fruit was used as a table decoration at elegant turn-of-the-century dinners like Samantha's. After the dessert course (and when all of the guests had lifted finger bowls off of their fruit plates), a servant passed the fancy fruit bowl and guests helped themselves.

Samantha used silver scissors to cut herself a bunch of grapes. There were also apples, pears, and oranges. Proper guests peeled these fruits with special fruit knives and ate them with fruit forks. Using fingers was considered impolite.

You can serve the same fresh fruits Samantha would have eaten. If you try to eat them the way every proper lady and gentleman did at the turn of the century, you'll understand why Samantha was so proud when Grandmary complimented her good manners.

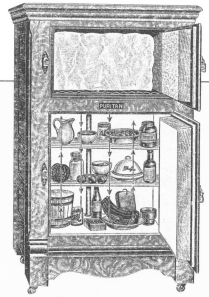

ICEBOXES

*Even the most modern turn-of-the-century kitchens didn't have electric refrigerators and freezers to store food like ice cream. But there were **iceboxes** to keep some food cool.*

An icebox was a wooden chest with room for food and a big block of ice. As the ice melted, it cooled the food in the icebox.

*Icebox ice was harvested from frozen lakes during the cold winter. It was shipped in trains, stored in buildings called **ice houses**, and delivered in wagons to homes like Samantha's.*

Chapter Three
MOLLY'S LUNCH

 For patriotic girls like Molly, packing a healthy lunch was a sure-fire way to help win World War Two. "Food is the mightiest weapon of them all," pamphlets and posters said to Americans who were hoping and working for victory. "FOOD FIGHTS FOR FREEDOM."

In 1944, thousands of American soldiers were fighting in faraway lands. Their families said they were fighting, too—on America's home front. On the home front, girls like Molly did everything they could for the war effort. They didn't waste metal or other materials needed for war equipment. They ate less meat, sugar, and canned vegetables so that there would be more to send to soldiers. And they grew their own fresh vegetables in Victory gardens.

Americans said "V is for Victory" during World War Two. V was also for Vigor and Vim—the pep that helped everyone on the home front do important wartime work. Home-front cooks understood that pep came from another big V—Vitamins. When Molly was a girl, more Americans than ever knew that good food and vitamins build healthy bodies with lots of get-up-and-go.

One of Molly's favorite vitamins was the imaginary vitamin Z. Lots of Z, for Zest, made Molly's lunch good to look at, good tasting, and fun to eat. Fresh vegetables from the Victory garden, peanut butter for protein, and a sugarless dessert made it good for her in 1944—and for you today!

MOLLY

MENU

Molly's Schoolday Lunch
September 1944

Deviled Eggs
•
Victory Garden Vegetable Soup
•
Sandwiches:
Hurray, Hurray for PBJ
Jelly Flags
Lettuce? Try It!
•
Carrot Curls
•
Celery Fans
•
Applesauce Cupcakes with
Cream Cheese Frosting
•
Milk
•
Fresh Fruit

THE BASIC SEVEN

During World War Two, meal-planning was the job of American women. Even "double-duty housewives," women who worked at home and at wartime jobs, were expected to use the government's Basic Seven Food Chart to plan healthy menus for every meal, every day, every week of the year. Experts said that breakfast was the best time to eat eggs, cereals, and citrus fruits like oranges. Dinner was the meal for protein and vegetables. Lunch, the meal in between, was the place to add any of the Basic Seven that were missing from breakfast and dinner.

MOLLY'S BASIC SEVEN

"A healthy America is a strong America!" said newsreels and posters in 1944. "U.S. NEEDS US STRONG. Eat the Basic Seven every day."

The Basic Seven were seven kinds of food. They were divided into food groups, **The Basic Seven Food Groups,** on a chart that government experts made to help home-front Americans plan good, healthy meals. "Include foods from each group in each day's meals—and you can't go wrong," the experts said.

Molly's lunch included every one of the Basic Seven. There was food from three different groups in Victory Garden Vegetable Soup. Leafy lettuce, green peas, and carrots came from Group One. Chunky tomatoes and their juice, which added lots of vitamin C, were from Group Two. Group Three vegetables—potatoes, corn, and turnips—helped out by adding more vitamins and minerals.

Since The Basic Seven Food Chart encouraged Americans to eat both raw and cooked vegetables, Molly's lunch also included crisp carrot curls from Group One and fancy celery fans from Group Three.

Group Four—milk and dairy products—was an important one for children, who were supposed to drink at least four glasses of milk a day. When children had meatless meals like Molly's schoolday lunch, experts said they needed even more dairy products. So the frosting on Molly's cupcakes was made with cream cheese.

Peanut butter was a Group Five food and a good source of protein. In the 1940s, protein that came from meat, fish, and eggs was called first-class protein. Second-class protein that came from plants like peanuts and soybeans worried some Americans, who thought only first-class protein could make them strong. The experts said that wasn't true, but Molly added a deviled egg to her lunch menu just in case.

Molly ate her peanut butter on sandwiches, and they were made with bread. Group Six of the Basic Seven included bread, flour, and cereals. Some home-front cooks *enriched* bread they baked at home by adding spinach or tomato juice to the dough. Their "pepped-up" bread had extra vitamins, but it was green or pink! Whole-wheat bread or white bread made from enriched flour was less colorful, but just as rich in vitamins.

Butter, margarine, and cooking oil were in short supply during World War Two, so Americans on the home front ate only small amounts of Group Seven foods. Molly spread butter very thin and used only a little mayonnaise, which was made with oil, when she prepared two of her lunchtime specialties, Jelly Flags and Lettuce? Try It! sandwiches.

DIVIDE YOUR DOLLAR

Americans who liked The Basic Seven Food Chart wanted an easy way to know how much of each group to eat. Experts told them to divide each dollar they spent on food this way:

- *30¢ or more for Groups One, Two, and Three*
- *20¢ or more for Group Four*
- *25¢ or less for Group Five*
- *15¢ or less for Group Six*
- *10¢ or less for Group Seven*

RATION POINTS

In stores, people paid money and points for food. Letters on ration stamps told when they could be used. Numbers told how many points they were worth.

Tokens were used to make change for ration points. Each token was worth a point. Red tokens made change for red stamps, blue for blue.

SHOPPING AND SHORTAGES

During World War Two, some foods were hard to get on the home front. Much of America's supply of sugar, coffee, meat, cheese, and butter was shipped to faraway places where United States troops were fighting or where America's allies needed food.

Canned food was easier to ship across an ocean than fresh food was. Fresh food spoiled and got squashed. Cans were easy to store. In places where there were no refrigerators, canned food didn't spoil. And canned food was easy to use. At mealtime, it could be heated and served. That was easy for soldier cooks and for double-duty housewives.

But metal for cans was scarce during World War Two. Factories were using all the steel and tin they could get for ships, tanks, guns, and bullets. In a short time, canned food became scarce on the home front. In some places, selfish "hoarding hogs" tried to buy all the canned food they could find and keep it for themselves.

To give every family on the home front a fair chance to get foods that were in short supply, the government started a system called **rationing**. Every man, woman, and child got a ration book full of red and blue stamps. The stamps were marked with numbers that told how many **points** they were worth. People had to use points *and* money to buy things that were rationed. Red points were for meat, cheese, sugar, butter, and oil. Blue points were for canned food. The number of points people could spend each month, and the number of points things cost, changed at different times during the war.

Rationing taught Americans on the home front to use scarce food and canned goods wisely. Families also learned to grow all the vegetables they needed in back-yard Victory gardens. They "canned" their Victory garden vegetables in glass jars. Some schools and factories set land aside for students and workers to use as Victory gardens, too. During World War Two, more than a million tons of vegetables a year were grown in Victory gardens. That was nearly half the vegetables home-front Americans ate.

"Waste during War is sabotage!" said wartime posters. Home-front families quickly learned that food wasn't the only thing that could be wasted. Time became precious, too. For women who went off to wartime jobs and still had work to do at home, time was especially scarce. So they asked their families for help in the kitchen. They also turned to cookbooks, which were filled with tips to make cooking and meal-planning quick and easy. Many wartime cookbooks gave a month's worth of menus that didn't use rationed food but did include the Basic Seven in every meal.

Call VEGETABLES INTO SERVICE

VICTORY WITH VEGETABLES

Home-front cooks were inspired by poems like this one, from a wartime cookbook.

A vegetable correctly cooked
Has color, health, and taste!
A vegetable that's murdered
In the pot is so much waste.
Use just a little water
And not too long a time—
Make your vegetables a perfect dish
And not a perfect crime!
—from "Coupon Cookery"

**If you pack a lunch box
keep these things in mind**

*A Good Lunch Must Nourish . . .
    it has a big job to do
A Good Lunch Must Taste Good . . .
    or it may not be eaten
A Good Lunch Must Carry Well . . .
    or it will be unappetizing*
        —*from the 1944
        "Health-for-Victory Meal
        Planning Guide"*

PACKING MOLLY'S LUNCH

Like most children growing up in 1944, Molly went to a school that was so close to her house, she could go home at noon for a hearty hot lunch. When she brought her lunch to school, Molly's sandwiches were wrapped in waxed paper. (Plastic sandwich bags hadn't been invented in 1944!) She carried Victory Garden Vegetable Soup in a thermos bottle with a cork stopper.

Your sandwiches will stay fresh in a waxed paper wrapper when you use a *drugstore wrap*.

 **1.** Place your sandwich in the center of a 12-inch square of waxed paper. Bring two edges together above the sandwich.

 **2.** Fold the edges over and over until the fold is flat against the sandwich. Press out air.

 **3.** Fold the open sides into triangles as shown.

 **4.** Fold the triangles under your sandwich. The weight of the sandwich will keep the wrapping closed.

DEVILED EGGS

Ingredients		Equipment
6 hard-boiled eggs	1/4 teaspoon salt	Knife
2 to 3 tablespoons mayonnaise	1/4 teaspoon pepper	Small mixing bowl
	Paprika	Plate
1 tablespoon pickle relish	Sliced pimento-stuffed olives	Fork
1 teaspoon prepared mustard		Measuring spoons
		2 spoons

Directions   *6 servings*

1. Follow Steps 1 through 3 on page 13 to make hard-boiled eggs.

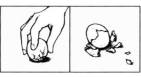

2. Tap each <u>egg</u> lightly against a hard surface until it is shattered all around. Then peel off the shell. ***Tip:*** *Peel gently so you don't tear the egg whites.*

3. Slice the egg in half lengthwise. Put <u>egg yolks</u> in the bowl. Put the <u>whites</u> onto a plate.

4. Mash the yolks with a fork. Stir in the <u>mayonnaise</u>, <u>relish</u>, <u>mustard</u>, <u>salt</u>, and <u>pepper</u>. Mix until smooth.

5. Use two spoons to carefully put the yolk mixture back into the whites.
Tip: *Try to fill each of the 12 halves equally.*

6. Sprinkle each deviled egg with a little <u>paprika</u>. Top with a slice of <u>olive</u>.

DEVILED EGGS

Pretty foods add zest to meals— and eggs are packed with protein, too.

In September 1944, eggs cost 51¢ a dozen.

VICTORY GARDEN VEGETABLE SOUP

Molly even liked the turnips in this thick tomato soup with chunks of fresh garden vegetables.

In 1944, families with large Victory gardens "canned" tomatoes and tomato juice in glass jars. Tomato juice in metal cans was rationed. In September 1944, a large can of tomato juice cost 21¢ and 40 points.

VICTORY GARDEN VEGETABLE SOUP

Ingredients

1 large potato	2 cups water
1 medium onion	1 tablespoon salt
2 ribs celery	1/4 teaspoon pepper
3 carrots	1/3 cup alphabet
2 medium turnips	macaroni
1 cup corn	
1 cup peas	
2 tomatoes	
5 lettuce leaves	
3 tablespoons butter	
3 tablespoons flour	
4 cups tomato juice	

Equipment

Vegetable peeler
Knife and cutting
  board
Small saucepan
Measuring cups and
  spoons
Kitchen shears
Fork
Sieve
Small bowl
Wooden spoon
Large soup pot

Directions

12 servings

1. Peel the <u>potato</u> and cut it into pieces. Put the pieces in the small saucepan. Cover them with cold water.

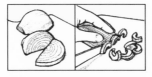

Tip: You can cut the potato into slices or "dice" it by cutting the slices into small blocks. The smaller the pieces, the faster the potato will cook.

2. Slice the <u>onion</u> and <u>celery</u>. Set them aside.

Tip: Peel the onion and cut it in half from top to bottom. Cut thin onion slices this way.
Tip: Wash the celery and slice it like this.

3. Prepare all the other vegetables.

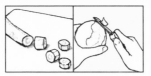

Tip: Peel the <u>carrots</u>. Slice them 1/2 inch thick.
Tip: Dice the <u>turnips</u>. Turnips from the store are sometimes waxed. Cut off the wax with a vegetable peeler.

Tip: Slice fresh <u>corn</u> from the cob like this—or use frozen corn.

Tip: Remove fresh <u>peas</u> from the pod—or use frozen peas.

Tip: Cut <u>tomatoes</u> in chunks.
Tip: Cut <u>lettuce</u> into 1-inch squares. Kitchen shears make this step easy.

4. Cook the <u>potato</u> pieces over medium-high heat. When the water begins to boil, turn the heat down to medium. Boil until the pieces break apart when you pierce them with a fork. While the potato pieces are cooking, place a sieve over a bowl. Drain the cooked potato pieces through a sieve and catch the liquid in the  bowl. Then press the cooked potato through the sieve into the bowl of liquid. Set it aside. *Tip: Use a wooden spoon to press the potato through the sieve.*

5. In the soup pot, melt the <u>butter</u> over medium heat. Add the <u>onion</u> and <u>celery</u>. Cook until they are soft, for about 10 minutes. Stir often.

6. Add the <u>flour</u> all at once. Stir for one minute. Then add the <u>tomato juice</u>, <u>2 cups water</u>, <u>salt</u>, <u>pepper</u>, and <u>macaroni</u>. Stir well.

7. Add the <u>potato</u> and <u>potato liquid</u>, <u>carrots</u>, <u>corn</u>, <u>peas</u>, <u>lettuce</u>, and <u>tomatoes</u>.

8. Cook the soup over medium heat, stirring occasionally. Just before it begins to boil, lower the heat. Simmer for 20 minutes. Serve hot. *Tip: You'll see only a few tiny bubbles along the side of the pot as the soup simmers.*

SOUP MEASUREMENTS

"Waste not, want not" was a popular home-front motto. Many of the ingredients in this recipe aren't measured in cups because vegetables aren't always the same size— and soup is not a place to make leftovers! In fact, clever home-front cooks often added leftovers from the refrigerator to their tasty soups.

If you measured, though, you would find about 1 cup of onions, 1 cup of celery, 1 cup of carrots, 1 cup of lettuce, and 1 cup of turnips in this recipe. But a little more of one vegetable and a little less of another won't hurt. You may even want to add other favorites of your own!

SANDWICHES

Hurray, Hurray for PBJ
Jelly Flags
Lettuce? Try It!

Variety was important in a Victory lunch. Here are new shapes for old favorites. Mix and match!

SANDWICHES

HURRAY, HURRAY FOR PBJ*

Ingredients	**Equipment**	
Thin-sliced enriched white bread	Sandwich spreader	Toothpicks
Your favorite peanut butter	Knife and cutting board	Waxed paper
Your favorite jelly		

* PBJ means peanut butter and jelly!

Directions

1. For each serving, use 2 pieces of <u>bread</u>. Spread each piece with <u>peanut butter</u>.

 **2.** Top the peanut butter with <u>jelly</u>. Trim off the crusts.

 **3.** Roll up each slice of bread, spread-side in. Fasten the rolls with toothpicks.
Tip: Use both hands to make even rolls.

4. Wrap the rolls in waxed paper and chill them in the refrigerator for 2 hours. *Tip: Twist the ends to keep the waxed paper closed over the rolls.*

5. When you're ready to eat, unwrap the rolls and slice across each one to make small pinwheels. Remove the toothpicks and serve sandwiches.
Tip: The rolls are easier to slice when they are cold.

JELLY FLAGS

Ingredients

Thin-sliced enriched
  white bread
Soft butter

Your favorite
  red jelly or jam

Equipment

Sandwich spreader
Knife and
  cutting board
Waxed paper

Directions

1. For each serving, spread a thin layer of <u>butter</u> on 3 pieces of

bread. Cover the butter with <u>jelly or jam</u>. Spread it thickly all the way to the edges.

2. Stack the slices one on top of the other. Top the stack with a piece of plain bread. Trim off the crusts.

3. Wrap the sandwiches in waxed paper and chill them in the refrigerator for 2 hours. *Tip: Use the drugstore wrap described on page 52.*

4. When you're ready to eat, unwrap and slice the stacked jelly bread into 4 strips. Turn them on their sides to make flags.
Tip: Chilling makes the sandwich easier to slice.

WARTIME SHOPPING LIST

September 1944

	cost	points
1 pound butter	46¢	16
1 pound margarine	39¢	4
1 pound peanut butter	25¢	0
1 pound grape jam	21¢	0
1 pound raspberry jam	31¢	0
1 loaf enriched bread	10¢	0

MORE PEANUT BUTTER FAVORITES

Since peanut butter wasn't rationed during World War Two, and it was a good source of protein, cookbooks had lots of ideas for peanut butter sandwiches. The "Pep Up" mixed peanut butter, honey, and compressed yeast (which added vitamins). There were also recipes for peanut butter and prune sandwiches and for mixtures of peanut butter and pickles, peanut butter and carrots, peanut butter and chili sauce, and peanut butter and beans.

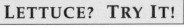

LETTUCE? TRY IT!

Ingredients		*Equipment*
Enriched whole-wheat bread	1/2 banana per sandwich	Sandwich spreader
Your favorite peanut butter	1 leaf of lettuce per sandwich	Knife and cutting board
Mayonnaise		Assorted cookie cutters

Directions

1. For each serving, use 2 pieces of <u>bread</u>. Spread <u>peanut butter</u> on one slice and <u>mayonnaise</u> on the other.

2. Slice the <u>banana</u>. Arrange banana slices on top of the peanut butter.

3. Cover the banana slices with <u>lettuce</u>. Top the sandwich with the mayonnaise bread.

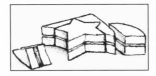

4. Use a sharp knife or a cookie cutter to cut the sandwich into a pretty shape.

Tip: Snack on the pieces you trim off—or feed them to the birds. Waste is sabotage!

CARROT CURLS AND CELERY FANS

Ingredients	Equipment	
3 large crisp carrots	Vegetable peeler	Large bowl of ice water
3 ribs of celery	Toothpicks	Knife

Directions   *6 servings*

1. Peel the <u>carrots</u>. Then use the peeler to make long, wide carrot slices.

2. Curl each carrot strip around your finger. Stick a toothpick through the curl to hold it together.

3. Soak the carrot curls in ice water for 1 hour. Remove toothpicks before serving. *Tip: An ice water bath helps the carrots keep their curls.*

4. Rinse the <u>celery</u> with cold water. Cut each rib into 3 pieces of equal length. Cut the pieces in half lengthwise to make sticks.

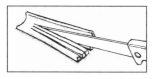

5. Cut 4 or 5 slits in each celery stick as shown. Soak the celery in ice water for 1 hour, or until the fans curl.

CARROT CURLS AND CELERY FANS

Fancy vegetable frills like these look tricky, but they're easy to make.

During World War Two, people spread peanut butter on celery, too.

APPLESAUCE CUPCAKES WITH CREAM CHEESE FROSTING

Molly made these delicious cup-cakes with cream cheese frosting even when eggs, sugar, and butter were in short supply.

Home-front cooks didn't spread frosting very thick. Sometimes they even served cupcakes without it!

APPLESAUCE CUPCAKES

Ingredients		Equipment
2 cups sifted flour	1 cup seedless	Cupcake or muffin
1 teaspoon	raisins	pans
baking soda	1/4 cup broken	16 paper cupcake
1/2 teaspoon	walnut pieces	liners
ground nutmeg		Measuring cups
1/2 teaspoon		and spoons
ground cinnamon		Sifter
1/4 teaspoon ground		Small bowl
cloves		Large mixing bowl
1/4 teaspoon salt		Rubber spatula
1/3 cup shortening		Electric mixer
3/4 cup honey		Wooden spoon
1 cup unsweetened		Toothpicks
applesauce		Wire cooling racks

Directions   *16 cupcakes*

1. Preheat the oven to 350°. Line the cupcake pans with paper liners.

2. In a small bowl, sift together the <u>flour</u>, <u>baking soda</u>, <u>nutmeg</u>, <u>cinnamon</u>, <u>cloves</u>, and <u>salt</u>. Set these dry ingredients aside.
Tip: Be sure to sift the flour twice—before you measure it, and then with the other dry ingredients.

3. Measure the <u>shortening</u> into the mixing bowl and beat at high speed until it is fluffy. *Tip: Use a rubber spatula to get the shortening out of the measuring cup.*

4. Add the <u>honey</u> and continue to beat the mixture for 2 minutes.
Tip: Stop the mixer once or twice and scrape down the sides of the bowl with the rubber spatula.

5. Add half the <u>applesauce</u> and half the sifted <u>dry ingredients</u> to the honey and shortening mixture. Mix at medium speed until all the flour disappears. Stop once or twice to scrape down the sides of the bowl.

6. Add the remaining <u>applesauce</u> and <u>dry ingredients</u>. Mix again until everything is blended. The batter will be thick. *Tip: Adding dry ingredients a little at a time keeps down "flour clouds."*

7. Stir in the <u>raisins</u> and <u>nuts</u>. *Tip: Use a wooden spoon, not the electric mixer, so that the raisins will stay whole.*

8. Spoon the batter into the cupcake pans.
Tip: Fill each cupcake liner 2/3 full, so that your cupcakes will have nice round tops.

9. Bake at 350° for 25 to 30 minutes.
Tip: Test cupcakes with a toothpick. Poke one in the center. If the toothpick comes out clean, your cupcakes are ready.

10. Take the pans from the oven and set them on wire racks to cool. After 10 minutes, take the cupcakes from the pans and let them finish cooling on the racks.

11. Frost the cupcakes when they are completely cool.

A PATRIOTIC POEM

In 1944, everyone on the home front was working for victory. As Molly and Mom planned a menu, they thought of this poem:

> *If Uncle Sam can carry food*
> *To all our fighting men—*
> *It's not too much for us to pack*
> *A lunchbox now and then.*
> *The mid-day meal must fight fatigue*
> *That's always somewhere lurkin'—*
> *It takes a tasty, hearty lunch*
> *To keep our workers workin'.*
> *—from "Coupon Cookery"*

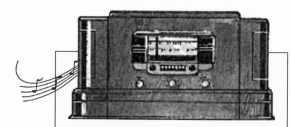

SONGS FOR KP

KP, for Kitchen Patrol, was the army word for cleanup. On the home front, singing along with the family or the radio made KP more fun. Check your library for records or tapes of old radio programs from the 1940s and play them the next time you're assigned to KP. Or see if anyone in your family can teach you to sing these songs that were hits in 1944:

> *"Sentimental Journey"*
> *"Swinging On a Star"*
> *"Don't Fence Me In"*

CREAM CHEESE FROSTING

Ingredients

2 ounces cream
  cheese at room
  temperature
5 tablespoons
  powdered sugar
1 tablespoon milk

1/2 teaspoon
  vanilla extract

Equipment

Electric mixer
Small bowl
Measuring cup
  and spoons
Sifter
Rubber spatula
Spreading knife

Directions

1. Beat the <u>cream cheese</u> with an electric mixer until it is soft and fluffy.

2. Sift the <u>powdered sugar</u>. Add the sifted powdered sugar to the cream cheese a little at a time. Beat the mixture each time you add more sugar. *Tip: Add the sugar slowly to keep down "clouds." Stop a few times and scrape down the sides of the bowl.*

3. Add the <u>milk</u> and <u>vanilla</u>. Beat until the frosting is smooth and creamy. *Tip: Add a little more powdered sugar if the frosting seems too wet. Add more milk, 1 teaspoon at a time, if it seems too dry.*

4. Frost the cupcakes.